Always remember...

You go girl!

You Go Girl
Personal Journal

Gray Tower Publishing

This page intentionally left blank

This page intentionally left blank